Blessed Are the Peacemakers

PEACE: freedom from war
strife. a treaty
agreement to end war
...dom from public dis-
turbance or disorder;
public security ; law and
order. FREEDOM from
...engagement, or ...
...mony ; concord
...an untroubled state
of mind; serenity, cal...
...from war).

Blessed Are the Peacemakers

Contemporary Thoughts
on Peace
Selected by Bill Webb
Illustrated by
Alexander Gsoell

Hallmark Editions

Blessed Are the Peacemakers

*Peace is when
time doesn't matter
as it passes by.*

Maria Schell

Make love not war

Howard Nemerov

make love not war

You may call for peace
as loudly as you wish,
but where there is
no brotherhood there can
in the end be no peace.

Max Lerner

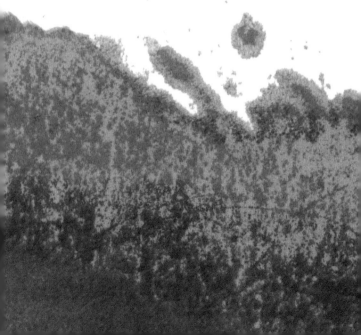

I think that the motive
that should guide all of us,
that should guide all
mankind, is to tame
the savageness of man
and make gentle the life
of the world.

Robert F. Kennedy

I believe that unarmed truth and unconditional love will have the final word in reality.

Dr. Martin Luther King, Jr.

Nonviolence is a weapon of the strong.

Mahatma Gandhi

Peace cannot be kept by force.
It can only be achieved
by understanding.

Albert Einstein

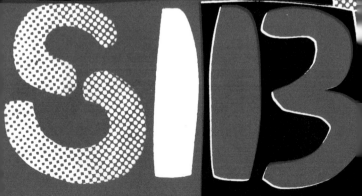

We are responsible to and for one another, and this responsibility is the ultimate claim imposed on all men alike.

Thomas A. Harris

No man's life is beautiful except in hurtless work.

Kenneth Patchen

*Nonviolence
is organized love.*

Joan Baez Harris

I do not want the peace
which passeth understanding,
I want the understanding
which bringeth peace.

Helen Keller

The dogmas of the quiet
past are inadequate
to the stormy present.

Abraham Lincoln

The human mind
can invent peace
with justice.

Norman Cousins

War is not healthy
          for children
and other living things.

Lorraine Schneider

Search for the next road
to peace— now, today.

Hermann Hesse

Peace will never happen
until we can laugh
at the stitches in our maps
where we think
we really split the planet
into parts....

Joseph Pintauro

*The time has now come
for man's intellect
to win out....*

Linus Pauling

There is no way to peace.
Peace is the way.

A. J. Muste

Sometime they'll give a war
and nobody will come.

Carl Sandburg

Love of my country
does not demand
that I shall hate
      and slay
those noble
      and faithful souls
who also love theirs.

Romain Rolland

Let peace begin with me.

Janice Jackson Miller